MY FIRST ENCYCLOPEDIA

An eye-catching series of information books designed to encourage young children to find out more about the world around them. Each one is carefully prepared by a subject specialist with the help of experienced writers and educational advisers.

KINGFISHER
Kingfisher Publications Plc
New Penderel House, 283-288 High Holborn, London WC1V 7HZ

First published in paperback by Kingfisher Publications Plc 1994
2 4 6 8 10 9 7 5 3 1
1BP/0500/SF/(FR)/135MA

Originally published in hardback under the series title Young World
This edition © copyright Kingfisher Publications Plc 2000
Text & Illustrations © copyright Kingfisher Publications Plc 1992

ISBN 1 85697 265 8

Phototypeset by Waveney Typesetters, Norwich
Printed in China

Plants

Kingfisher

Author
Fabienne Fustec

Botanical advisers
Denise Larpin and Jean-Noël Labat

Translator
Pat Pailing

Series consultant
Brian Williams

Editor
Véronique Herbold

Designer
Christian Beylier

Illustrators
Bernard Duhem
Catherine Fichaux
Pierre Hezard
Eva Styner

About this book

Millions of years ago, before the first animals appeared, there were plants on the Earth. Today there are plants almost everywhere – from the cold tundra regions to the hottest deserts. The biggest living things are plants, and the oldest ones too.

This book explains how plants grow and how much we depend on plants. It shows us the main sorts of plants, from the giant sequoia tree in the forest to the pot plant on the windowsill, from seaweed to apples and onions. By understanding them, we can learn how to look after the plants that share our world.

CONTENTS

PLANTS TO DISCOVER

THE LIVES OF PLANTS

ALL KINDS OF PLANTS

PLANTS FOR FUN

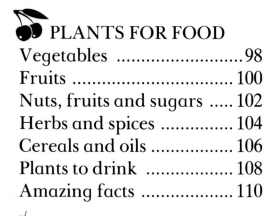

Plants

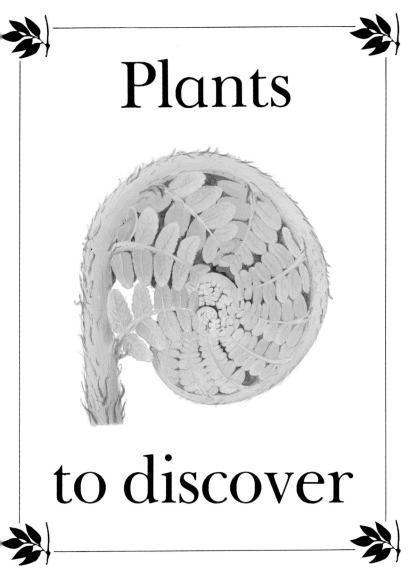

to discover

 # All around us

To discover the amazing world of plants, we just have to look around us.

We are surrounded by plants – plants in the country, at the seaside, in the city, or high up in the mountains. Plants of every size and shape and colour live in these places.

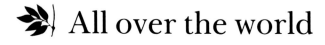

All over the world

Andes mountains

Sahara desert

People live in many places and dress and feed themselves according to where they live.

Plants are like that too. They live in many regions.

Amazon forest

But some plants survive in places where we cannot.

A type of crowfoot lives high up around glaciers in the Alps. Seaweed grows under water. The yucca lives in the hot, dry Arizona desert.

crowfoot

seaweed

yucca

15

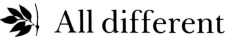 All different

Plants come in all sorts
of shapes and sizes.
Look at the
difference between
tiny duckweed . . .

duckweed

tree

. . . and a huge tree
with branches, roots
and a thick trunk! Or
a daffodil with long
leaves and a round
bulb, and a fern with
no flowers.

ferns   daffodils

Some plants do not have roots in soil. Epiphyte is the name for any plant that grows perched on other plants. This epiphyte is growing on a tree.

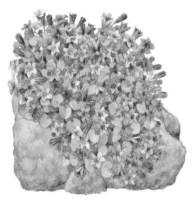

Brightly coloured bellflowers grow between the stones of a wall.

Palm trees have no branches. Marks on the trunks show where the old, dead leaves have fallen off.

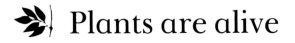 Plants are alive

Like all living things, plants need food to give them energy. Plants make their own food. Their roots take water from the soil, and their leaves take a gas called carbon dioxide from the air.

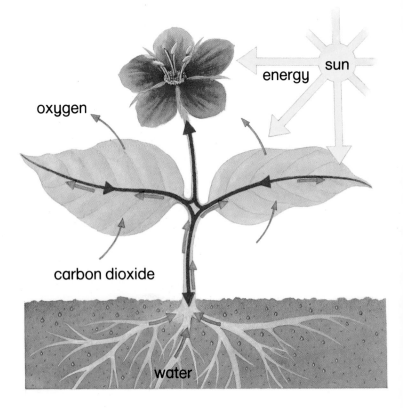

The water travels up the stem to the leaves, which contain a green chemical called chlorophyll. The chlorophyll uses carbon dioxide and sunlight to change the water from the roots into sugar. This process is called photosynthesis. The sugar feeds the whole plant.

Plants give off another gas, called oxygen, during photosynthesis. Plants use some of this oxygen for breathing, just as people and animals do. Plants sweat too. Some of the water soaked up by the roots is given off by the leaves. You can see this water inside a greenhouse or a bell-jar.

 # What plants need

To see how a plant takes water from the roots up to the leaves and around the whole plant, you can try this experiment. Use red food colouring to colour the water in a vase, and put a white flower in it.

carnation

A few hours later, the coloured water will have changed the colour of the flower. That is because the water has moved up the stem and into the leaves and flowers, through tiny tubes called veins.

Plants need light, water and air. With these three things, plants can live in a pot of soil.

anemones

cyclamen

pansies

Cut flowers can survive in water, but only for a few days. Left in the dark, or uprooted from their moist soil, plants wither and die.

 Clever plants

Plants develop weapons to protect themselves. They can repel animals and people who threaten their lives.

The nettle has hairs that sting.

The fly agaric is poisonous.

Do not touch!

Rose thorns prick.

Holly scratches.

So does the cactus.

22

Some plants need
insects to help them
produce new plants.
They attract
the insects
with smells.
(You can find out how
insects help plants
on page 37.)

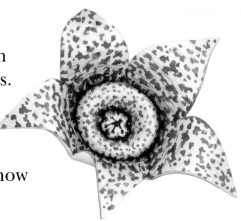

The stapelia has a
smell of rotting meat
that attracts flies.

Lilac gives off a
sweeter, nicer
scent!

The flower of the
bee orchid looks
and smells like a
bee. So real bees
sometimes come to
investigate.

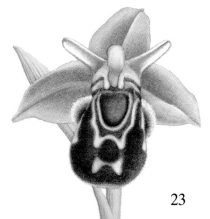

 Plants can adapt

Many plants live in very difficult environments, or surroundings. Very slowly, over thousands of years, they change to suit their environments. The changes are called adaptation.

The saguaro cactus stores water in its thick stems, to survive in the desert.

The water crowfoot has two kinds of leaves. Under the water, finely divided leaves let water flow through easily. On the surface, bigger leaves catch the sunlight.

Gunnera leaves are very large, up to three metres across. So they catch a lot of sunlight for photosynthesis.

The little leaves of the dwarf hebe are thick and juicy, because they store water.

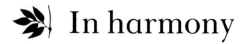 # In harmony

Mangrove trees
grow in swamps near the
sea, where the tide rises
and falls. Their long,
tangled roots anchor the
trees firmly in the mud,
and keep them above
water at high tide.

The sticky buds of the horse chestnut tree are covered in scales to protect them from cold winter winds.

Climbers are long, straggly plants that clamber up trees to reach the sunlight.

Epiphytes just perch on other plants.

The history of plants

In prehistoric times, before there were people, plants looked different. Some of these plants have left their imprints on rocks. The imprints are known as fossils. They give us clues about the plants of long ago.

Later, people began to use plants.

Papyrus reeds grow by the water. Papyrus was used as paper 6,000 years ago in Egypt.

Farmers have grown vines for about 5,000 years. Their grapes are used to make wine.

Maize grew in Mexico 4,000 years ago. Farmers still grow it for food today.

Amazing facts

Nearly all plants are green, because their leaves contain the green chemical called chlorophyll.

Trees release a lot of the oxygen we need to breathe and stay alive. So forests are often described as the lungs of the Earth.

Bamboo is the fastest growing plant in the world. It can grow as much as 90 centimetres in one day.

In the desert, the ocotillo bush drops all its leaves during the dry season. It grows more leaves as soon as it rains.

The raffia palm of Africa has very long leaves which may measure up to 25 metres. People use the leaves to weave hats, mats and baskets.

The lives

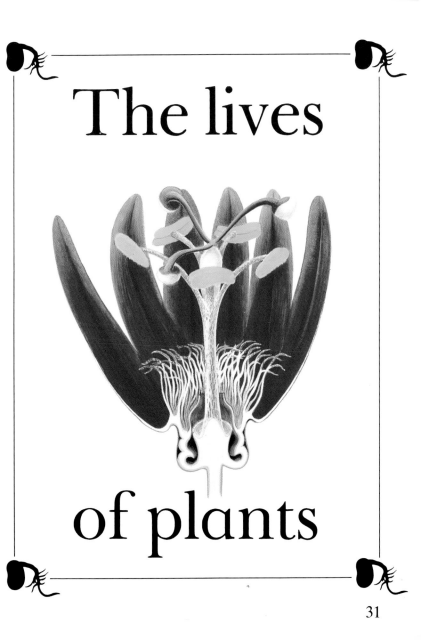

# of plants

The age of plants

Plants do not all live for the same amount of time. There are plants that live for just a few months or even weeks. After they have produced flowers, seeds and fruit, they die. These plants are called annuals.

Perennial plants live for several years. They usually have several crops of flowers, fruit and seeds before they die.

annuals

perennials

Some desert plants
appear after the
rains, and survive
for only a few
weeks.

dragon tree

The dragon tree,
the bristlecone
pine and the
yew live for
thousands
of years.

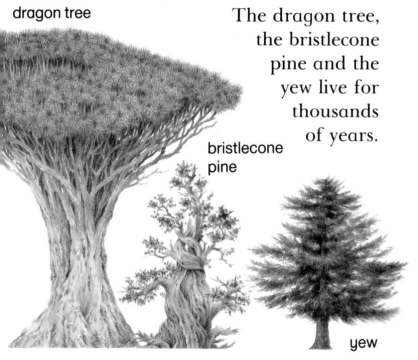

bristlecone
pine

yew

33

Reproduction

Many plants have flowers. Flowers make the seeds that grow new plants. Each flower has male parts, the stamens, and female parts, the carpels. Petals protect these parts.

If you look closely, you'll see that the centre of a sunflower has many small flowers.

stigma (part of carpel)

sunflower

lords-and-ladies

The stamens of lords-and-ladies are hidden in a white sheath called a spathe.

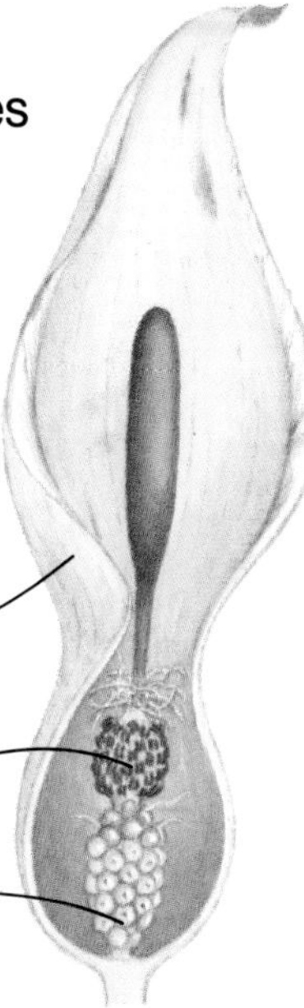

spathe

stamens

carpels

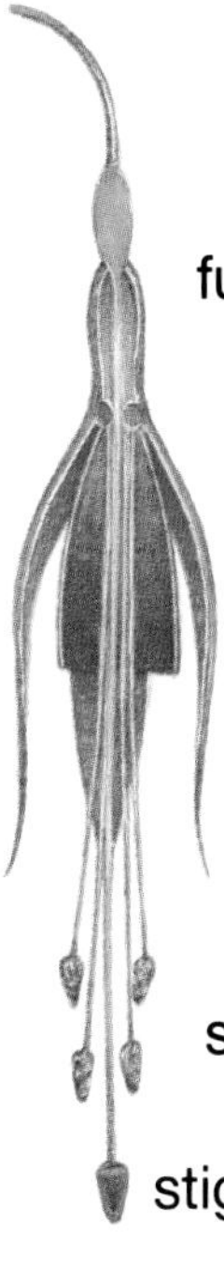

fuchsia

petal

The stamens of the fuchsia and the lily are easy to see.

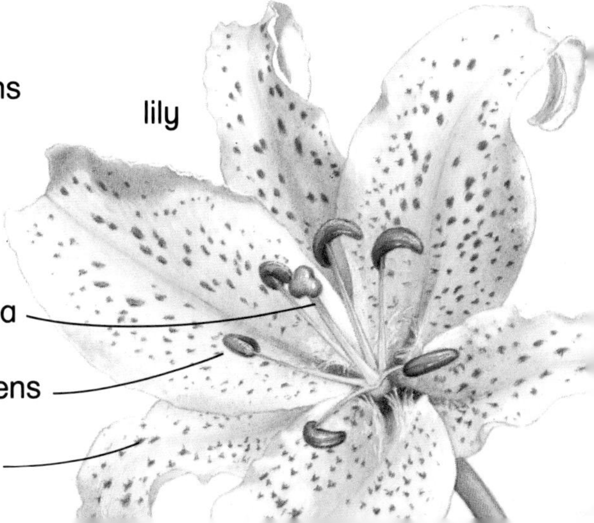

stamens

stigma

lily

stigma

stamens

petal

 Pollen

A flower's stamens produce tiny grains of pollen. The carpel contains eggs called ovules. For a plant to make seeds, the pollen has to reach the ovules. This is called pollination. It takes place in several ways.

Pine trees make pollen in little yellow cones instead of in flowers. The wind blows the pollen to ovules which are in red cones.

In some flowers, pollination takes place between the stamens and carpel of the same flower, before it opens. This is known as self-pollination.

Animals help to pollinate flowers. This bee is attracted by the bright colour and sweet smell of the dog-rose. Pollen sticks to the bee's furry body on one flower, and brushes off on another flower.

Many flowers also have a sweet liquid called nectar that attracts bees and other insects.

From flower to fruit

After the pollen becomes attached to the carpel and reaches the ovules inside, the eggs produce seeds. A fruit develops around the seed, sometimes around several seeds. The petals begin to drop off.

Rose hips are the fruits of the dog-rose. They contain lots of small seeds.

Pears contain seeds called pips.

The pumpkin plant has male and female flowers. After pollination, the female flower grows a fruit called a berry.

The berry grows into a big pumpkin, containing lots of seeds.

 Seeds

The fruit protects the seeds while they grow.

Some fruits contain a single seed inside a hard stone. Other fruits have several seeds called pips in their juicy pulp.

FRUITS WITH STONES

mango

sloes

peach

avocado

FRUITS WITH PIPS

pomegranate

kiwi fruit

bilberries

passion fruit

40

A strawberry has lots of pips. Each pip contains one seed.

Calabashes, or bottle gourds, are large, tough fruits that are used to hold water in Africa.

Nuts are seeds covered by a hard shell.

The poppy holds its seeds inside a case with a lid.

41

Ready for a journey

Seeds need to reach the ground before they can grow into new plants.

Dandelion seeds are scattered by the wind. Honesty seeds are flung out when the pods burst open.

If acorns are forgotten by the squirrel that buried them, they start to grow.

Coconuts sometimes fall into water and float a long way before reaching land.

The seeds of the wallaba do not travel far.
They fall straight to the ground when the pods open.

When birds eat fruit, they either spit out the seeds or swallow them. The seeds they swallow pass through their bodies and reach the ground in bird droppings.

Some fruits have tiny hooks and spines that stick to animals. Animals may carry these burrs a long way before they fall off.

Germination

When seeds are buried in soil and watered, they begin to swell. A baby plant bursts out of each one. This is called germination.

Here is the germination of a broad bean. The bean is a seed. A small root appears first and grows downwards. Then the leafy shoot pushes up into the light.

Some seeds send up one or two leaves called seed leaves or cotyledons before the shoot appears.
But the broad bean's seed leaves stay under-ground, in the seed.

Broad beans are delicious to eat. But beans from the pod can also be used to grow new plants.

The gardener makes a trench in the soil, puts in the beans and covers them. Then she waters the soil.

In warm weather, the beans take just a few days to germinate.

Plants without seeds

The whole process of growing new plants is called reproduction. But plants do not all reproduce with seeds. Some use their roots, or their bulbs, or their stems.

The tulip grows a new plant from a bulb.

The iris grows new plants from its underground stem every year. The stem is called a rhizome.

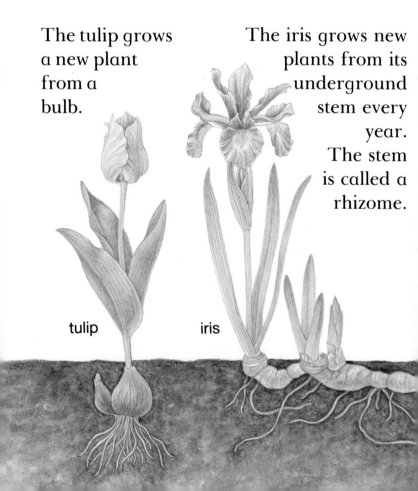

tulip

iris

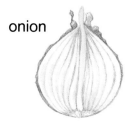

onion

The layers of an onion bulb are the young stem and leaves.

cassava

The strawberry plant sends out runners which take root and produce new plants.

strawberry

The cassava plant sprouts up from tubers.

Tubers are underground stems full of food.

A garden indoors

In winter, we can watch flowers growing safe in the warmth of our homes. Put some bulbs in a pot of clay pellets or soil, and water them from time to time.

fritillary

Put the pot in a sunny place when the flowers start to open.

crocus

tulip

You can sow parsley seed in pots all the year round.

If it is kept in a light, warm spot, the parsley will not be harmed by frost.

Protected by a greenhouse, orchids open out in the light at any time of the year.

🐿 The four seasons

In winter, many plants lose their flowers and their leaves. New leaves and flowers appear in spring, when it is warmer.

winter   spring

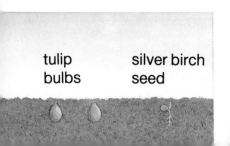

tulip   silver birch
bulbs   seed

In summer, fruits appear. In autumn, some trees change colour as their leaves turn yellow, red or brown and start to fall.

summer   autumn

Other seasons

Many parts of the world have four seasons. The weather changes, and this affects the way plants grow.

But not all parts of the world have four seasons. In the tropical forests around the Equator, it is always hot, and there is plenty of rain. So these forests are always green.

In the desert, there is a long dry season and a short rainy season.

As soon as it rains, some plants sprout up, burst into flower and make seeds, all in just a few days. Then they die. Their seeds lie buried in the ground, waiting for the next rainy season. Above ground, cactus plants survive by storing water in their thick, juicy leaves.

Amazing facts

🖤 As well as annuals and perennials, there are biennials. Biennials grow leaves in their first year, and flowers, fruits and seeds in their second year. Then they die.

🖤 In tropical countries, bats and humming-birds pollinate certain flowers when they come to drink their nectar.

🖤 The largest seeds in the world come from the coco-de-mer tree. One nut can weigh as much as 18 kilograms.

🖤 The seeds of the lotus can germinate even after waiting for several centuries. But those of the cacao tree die after a few days.

🖤 In the Galapagos Islands, there is a tomato whose seeds germinate only if they are swallowed by a giant tortoise. They pass through the tortoise and fall to the ground in its droppings.

All kinds of

plants

 # Flowers

The shapes of flowers vary.

Flowers are called regular if they have
identical petals. St John's-wort is regular.
The bellflower is also regular. Its petals
form a tube like a bell.

The toadflax is irregular, because the
petals are of unequal size and shape.

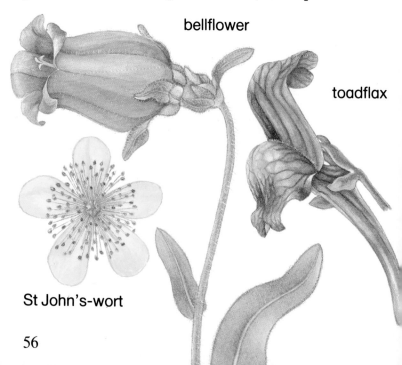

bellflower

toadflax

St John's-wort

The way flowers grow on plants also varies.

If flowers all grow from the same point at the top of a stem, the cluster is called an umbel. Wild celery has umbellate flowers.

Dahlias are composite flowers. Each head has masses of very small flowers, packed tightly together.

The lily-of-the-valley has little bells arranged along a long stem.

wild celery   lily-of-the-valley

dahlia

# Water plants

Water plants grow in rivers, ponds, pools and lakes. Usually, their roots are anchored in mud on the bottom, and their stems grow up to the surface of the water where the leaves and flowers open out.

The Amazon water lily has huge, flat leaves that grow as big as two metres across. These lilypads float on the surface of the water. Reeds and bulrushes have tall, narrow leaves.

water lily

Underwater plants often
have very fine leaves.

bulrush

water-milfoil

So the water can flow
past without battering
the plant.

 # Weird and wonderful

Here are some spectacular plants. The flowers of the canna are enclosed in large, colourful leaves called bracts.

The flower of the Dutchman's pipe has a pouch which attracts flies with its smell of rotting fish.

canna

Dutchman's pipe

The leaves of plants called living-stones look
like pebbles, so animals don't eat them.

The pitcher plant feeds on insects.
Its leaves are shaped like vases, with a flap
at the top to keep the rain out. Insects are
attracted by nectar around the rim, but
they fall down the slippery sides and drown
in a pool of liquid at the bottom. Then
the liquid digests the insects.

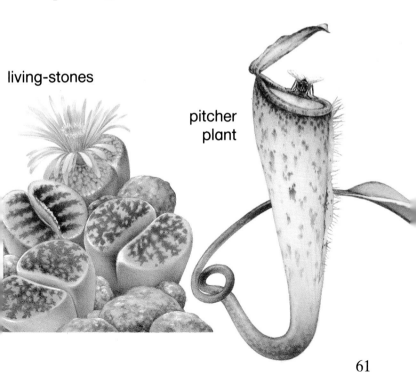

living-stones

pitcher
plant

 # Strange trees

The giant sequoia is one of the world's biggest trees. It can live for more than 2,000 years and measure over 80 metres tall.

The bottle tree is well named. Its trunk is shaped like a bottle and stores water, which is scarce in the desert where it lives.

giant sequoia

bottle tree

The amazing root of the mandrake can look a bit like a human body.

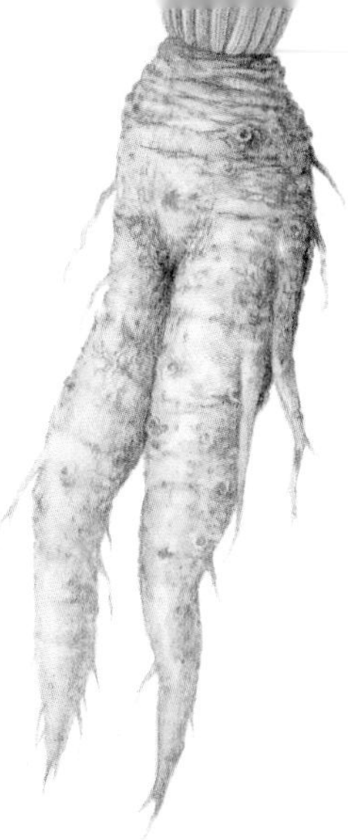

mandrake

Some roots of the swamp cypress come up above the surface of the waterlogged soil to breathe.

swamp cypress

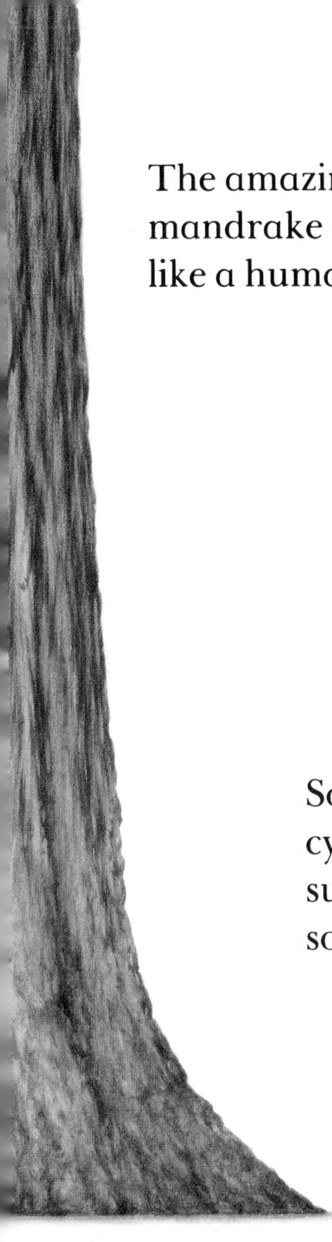

Studying plants

Botanists are scientists who study plants. They reckon there are about 350,000 species or kinds of plants. They sort species into groups, according to their similarities: what they look like, their way of life, and so on. This is called classification.

Algae live in all kinds of water.

Fungi have no chlorophyll.

Lichen is a fungus . . .

NON-FLOWERING PLANTS

. . . combined with an alga.

Mosses and ferns reproduce with spores.

Conifers are trees that have cones.

FLOWERING PLANTS

Many flowering plants have soft stems.

Climbers have long twisting stems.

Trees are usually large, with thick trunks of wood.

Shrubs are smaller.

Algae

Algae are nearly all water plants. But there are some that are found on land. Algae may be so small that they can be seen only under a microscope. Or they may be several metres long, like the seaweed in this picture. They do not have any roots.

Algae can be blue, red, green or brown, but they all contain chlorophyll for making food, and they all need sunlight.

Many algae form long green strands in ponds.

This is what they look like when you see them through a microscope.

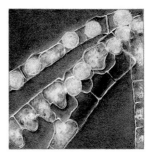

Some microscopic algae can swim towards the light by wiggling their tails.

 # Fungi

Fungi have no leaves, stems or roots, and they have no chlorophyll. They get their food from roots and dead leaves in the soil and from the plants they grow on.

chanterelle   morel

Do not pick or even touch fungi. Some can kill you.

cage fungus   devil's fingers

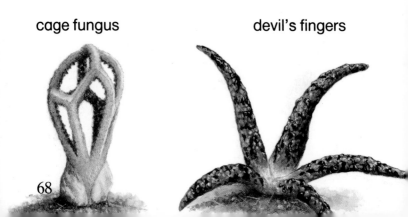

68

The moulds that can appear on cheese and old jam are tiny fungi. The medicine penicillin is obtained from moulds like these.

penicillium mould

puff-ball

Fungi reproduce with spores instead of seeds. The puff-ball releases millions of tiny spores like specks of dust.

beefsteak

The beefsteak fungus grows on tree trunks.

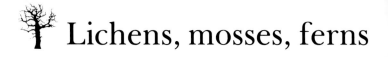 Lichens, mosses, ferns

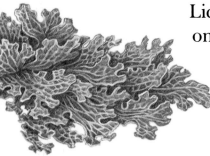

Lichen grows very slowly
on soil, trees and stones.
Some lichens live for
4,000 years.

Moss grows in damp
places. It is made up of
tiny stems and leaves.

Lichens, mosses and
ferns reproduce with
spores.

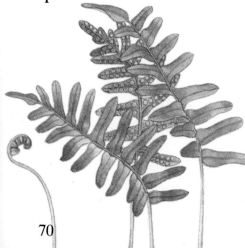

Fern leaves are
tightly coiled when
they are young.
After they unfold,
little brown spores
underneath drop
to the ground.

 # Conifers

The trees known as conifers bear seeds in cones. The cones are usually hard like wood, but some are small and soft like berries.

Cones take a long time to ripen. When they open, the winged seeds inside drift away on the breeze.

larch

spruce

Nootka cypress

Conifers have narrow, sharp leaves called needles. Most conifers keep their leaves all year, so we call them evergreen.

There have been ginkgo trees since prehistoric times. They are related to conifers.

weeping sequoia

73

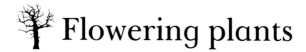 Flowering plants

Flowering plants have
two main kinds of leaves.

Plants which emerge from their seeds with
one cotyledon, or seed leaf, have leaves with
veins in parallel lines.

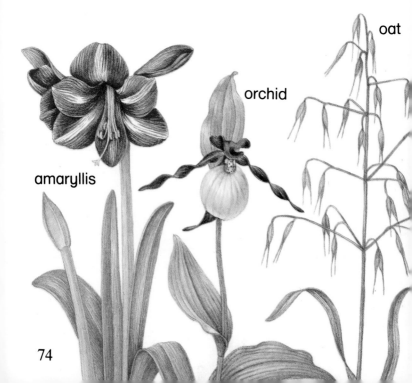

oat

orchid

amaryllis

Plants with two cotyledons have leaves with
a network of veins.

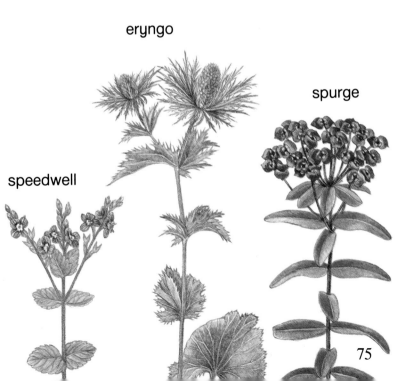

speedwell

eryngo

spurge

75

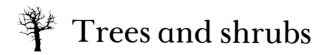# Trees and shrubs

Most trees, shrubs and climbers grow flowers. The magnolia, rhododendron and passion flower all have beautiful blossoms.

Bark is the tree's skin. It is dead wood, dry and tough, and it protects the living wood it covers.

Every year, a new ring of wood grows under the bark.

The heart-wood in the centre of the trunk is the oldest wood.

magnolia

rhododendron

bark

new growth

heart-wood

passion flower

Many trees shed their leaves in autumn, and grow new leaves in spring. They are called deciduous trees.

maple

spring
colour

autumn
colour

77

Plants for life

Plants are an essential part of life.

- Plants use energy from the sun to grow.
- Plants are food for animals.
- Animal droppings, and the remains of dead plants and animals, are taken into the soil by insects and worms.
- Soil provides some food for plants.

The panda depends on bamboo, because it eats little else.

Trees are
habitats.
That means
they are homes
for other plants
and animals.

One oak tree
may have 400
species living
on it.

# Forests at risk

A forest fire is a disaster because it destroys trees and a habitat for wildlife.

When a fire breaks out, fire-fighting aircraft spray water over the forest to put out the flames.

Many forests are being
destroyed to provide timber and
make room for farmland. Trees
take a long time to grow, so we
cannot replace the forests easily.
We must look after them.

Plants in danger

Fires, pollution and building new roads and towns damage the places where plants live. So some plants are in danger of becoming extinct. That means they may die out and disappear for ever. These are some endangered plants.

Venus flytrap

corn cockle

chickweed-wintergreen

Geissorhiza radians

eucalyptus

Nature reserves are areas set aside to protect wildlife. Picking flowers, cutting down trees, or doing anything that damages their habitat is forbidden.

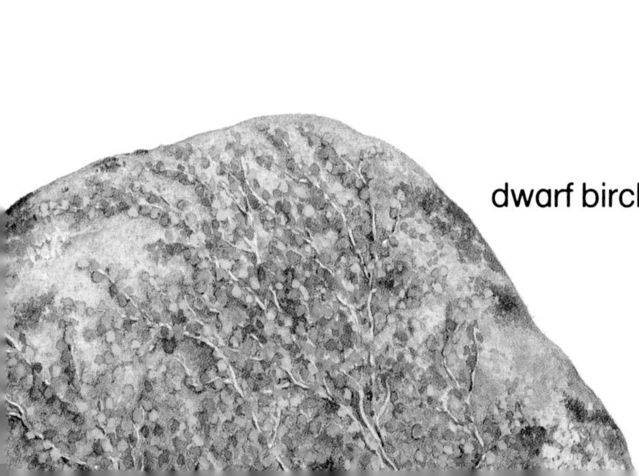

dwarf birch

Amazing facts

The largest flowers in the world belong to the rafflesia. A flower can be one metre wide and weigh almost seven kilograms.

The smallest flowering plant in the world is the Brazilian duckweed. Its flowers measure half a millimetre across.

Giant sequoias are over 80 metres high. The biggest weigh over 6,000 tonnes. These trees are the largest living things ever.

The smallest tree is the snow willow. It grows in cracks in the rock, in the frozen Arctic. It is only a few centimetres high, and its trunk is as thin as a pencil.

At least 400 species of plants become extinct every year.

Plants

for fun

House plants

Many plants are easy to grow indoors as long as they have light, soil and water.

House plants can have beautiful flowers or leaves. They are usually easy to look after too.

Small plants can
be used to make a
miniature garden.

A balcony is a good place for big plants.
But some plants are delicate. They need
to be kept indoors, away from cold winds
and rain.

☙ New plants

We can replace an old plant by using parts of it to grow new ones. Gardeners call this propagation.

The spider plant grows young plants on the end of long stems. These plantlets take root when they are put in a pot of soil.

For some plants, if a leaf is placed in soil, it will produce a plantlet. This is known as a leaf cutting.

In spring, an ivy stem left in a jar of water will grow roots. Then it can be planted.

Suckers grow from the main stem or root of a plant. If they are taken off and put in a pot, they will produce new plants.

The stems of some plants form clumps. These can be divided and planted separately.

🪣 Healthy plants

Some insects and fungi are harmful to plants. Mealy bugs are insects that attack the cactus. Blackspot is a fungus that damages the leaves of roses.

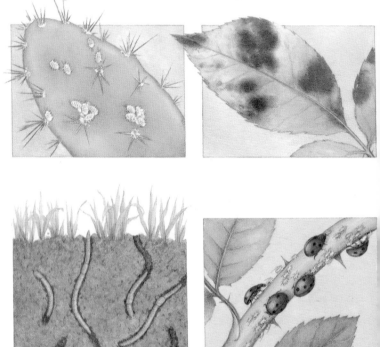

On the other hand, many small creatures are useful. Worms make tunnels that let air into the soil. Ladybirds eat harmful aphids.

Pot plants need care.

Pebbles in the bottom of the pot let water drain away from the soil, to prevent the roots rotting in too much water.

If you are away for a week or two on holiday, a wick will carry water from a bottle to the plant.

If the air is too hot or dry, it is often a good idea to spray the leaves with water.

🪣 Plants for decoration

To make them last longer, cut flowers can be dried by hanging them upside down.

These fruits are ornamental gourds. Gardeners grow them for their shape and colours, not to eat.

Making beautiful flower
arrangements is an art.
We can use fresh flowers,
dried flowers, interesting
grasses and leaves –
almost anything.

93

🜂 Plants to keep

Many plants smell nice. We can fill sachets and jars with shavings of wood such as sandalwood, citrus fruit peel, dried petals, powdered orris root, spices and herbs. These all perfume cupboards and rooms.

Plants are used to make perfumes. Their scent is often added to soap and candles. Roses are very popular.

citrus peel

cinnamon

lavender

orris root

damask rose

To preserve plants and learn to recognize them, you can pick some (only a few), dry them and stick them onto sheets of paper. Collect the sheets and make a book. An album of plants is called a herbarium.

To flatten and dry the flowers, you simply put them into a flower press.

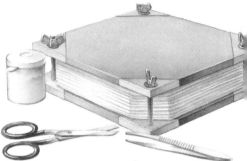

One month later, you can arrange the flowers and fix them in place with sticky tape. Write down the name of the flower, and the date and place where you found it.

Amazing facts

Flowers open at different times of the day. The geranium opens in the morning, the marvel-of-Peru in the evening.

The desert rose is made from grains of sand hardened by winds and desert frosts into shapes like the petals of a rose.

People have invented a language of flowers: they say the lily-of-the-valley brings good luck, and a red rose signifies love.

The bonsai is a minature tree. In Japanese, the name means "to plant in shallow dishes".

Pomanders are used to perfume cupboards. A pomander is an orange studded with cloves and rolled in spices.

100,000 roses are needed to obtain one litre of rose oil.

Plants

for food

🍒 Vegetables

potato

lettuce

carrot

Here are some of the vegetables we grow for food. We eat several parts: the leaves of the lettuce, the roots of carrots, the tubers of potatoes, the flowers of cauliflowers, the stalks of spinach beet and the pods of French beans, but the seeds of broad beans.

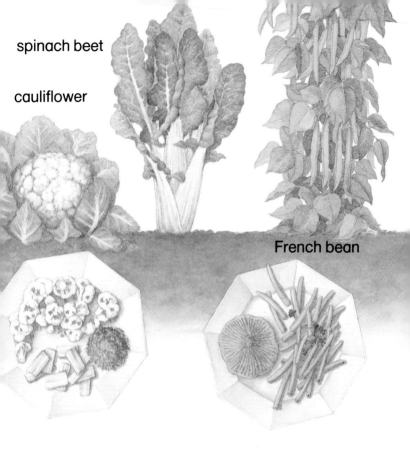

spinach beet

cauliflower

French bean

Vegetables taste good, and they provide us
with vitamins and minerals that keep us
healthy. We eat raw vegetables, grated
or cut into slices. And we eat cooked
vegetables in many ways – sliced,
mashed or with a sauce.

99

 Fruits

Like vegetables, fruit is delicious and healthy.

Tomatoes are often called vegetables, but they are in fact a fruit.

When its shell is broken open, the coconut can be eaten fresh with its milk, or dried and grated.

The prickly pear is nice to eat but not to pick!

Bananas grow in
bunches. They turn from
green to yellow as they
ripen.

Oranges contain lots of
vitamin C.

🍒 Nuts, fruits and sugars

Most fruits are ready to eat in the summer. Hard shells preserve nuts for a long time. So we can eat nuts during the winter.

We can eat summer fruits all year round if they have been dried.

In jam, salads and cakes, fruit is delicious to eat!

Sugar comes from the root of sugar beet.

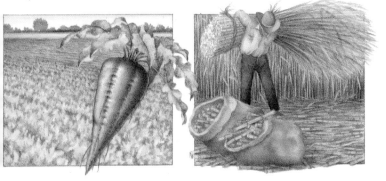

Sugar also comes from sugar cane grown in hot countries. The stems are cut down and crushed, and their juice is used to make sugar.

Bees gather nectar from flowers and turn it into honey.

🍒 Herbs and spices

Cooks use plants called herbs to add flavour to food. Sometimes the herbs are freshly cut, sometimes they are dried.

thyme   bay leaf   basil

mint   coriander   tarragon

These plants are also used to make herbal teas.

Spices also add flavour to food.

Some spices are very hot, such as chilli peppers. Others are mild and sweet, such as vanilla. We use their fruits, stems, roots, dried flowers and seeds.

vanilla pods,
the fruits of an orchid

1) peppers
2) cinnamon
3) ginger
4) nutmeg
5) cloves
6) peppercorns
7) turmeric
8) saffron

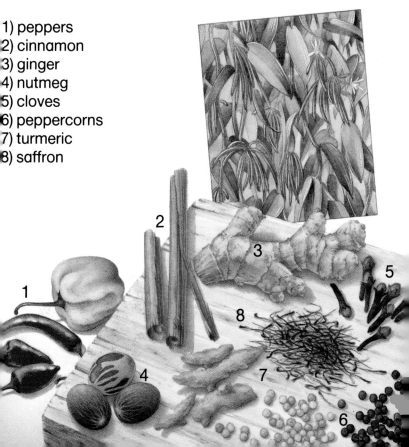

 Cereals and oils

Cereals are grown for their seeds or grains.
Some grains are turned into flour, to make
bread. Some are used in breakfast cereals.
And farmers feed some grains to their
animals.

wheat   maize   rice   millet

The fruits and seeds of certain plants
provide vegetable oils. Vegetable oils
contain some of the vitamins we need.
And we use them for cooking.

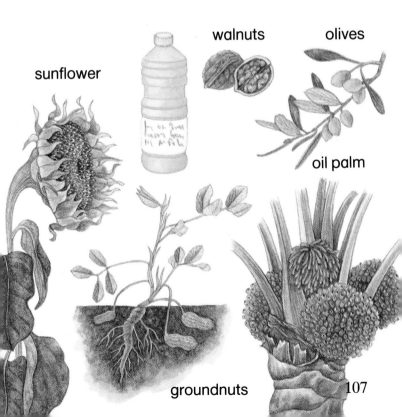

sunflower

walnuts

olives

oil palm

groundnuts

107

 Plants to drink

If we squeeze the juice from fruit, we can make delicious drinks. Or we can mix fruit and milk or ice cream in a blender, to make a milkshake.

Coffee is made from the beans of the coffee plant.

Tea comes from the leaves of tea plants.

Chocolate is made from the fruits of the cacao-tree, which are called cacao-pods.

The seeds, or cacao beans, inside the pod are taken out, dried and roasted.

Then the beans are crushed to produce cocoa powder. We can heat cocoa with milk and sugar, to make a mug of drinking chocolate.

Amazing facts

The 'eyes' of a potato are really the small buds that send up leafy shoots if the potato is planted.

Soya beans are a vegetable, but they can be cooked to look and taste like meat. They contain lots of protein.

The heaviest orange ever reported weighed two and a half kilograms. It was as big as your head!

More people eat rice than any other kind of food. It is the main food for more than half of the world's population.

For thousands of years, the people of Japan have eaten seaweed.

Useful

plants

☙ Health and beauty

Many medicines and health products are made from plants. Lotions made with arnic are good for bruises. Dandelion juice is put on warts. Lime-blossom tea helps us feel relaxed. Lemon-balm cordial is soothing too.

arnica

dandelion

lime

lemon balm

Beauty products are often made from plants, like this home-made cucumber face mask.

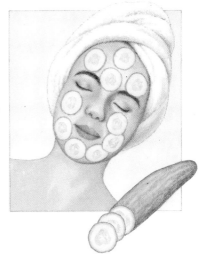

Indians in the Amazon forests use plant dyes to paint their bodies. The seed of the annatto tree produces a red dye that colours their skin and hair, and protects them against insect bites.

🐾 Plants for timber

Trees provide timber for building houses and making furniture. The cork oak's bark is used to make cork floor tiles.

The strong stems of the bamboo are used to build fences and houses.

The stems of the rattan palm are used to make cane furniture.

Baskets are woven from the flexible branches of a willow tree called the osier.

The future of plants

All over the world, botanists are studying plants and their habitats. They try to learn more about plants, so that they can protect them and find new ways of using them for food and medicine.

This expedition is studying plants in the rainforest.

Scientists are trying to develop new plants that can survive in places where it is difficult to grow enough food.

They can now grow plants without soil, by spraying a mixture of water and fertilizer onto the roots.

A super-carrot with lots of vitamin A is being created for countries where people do not have enough to eat.

Plants for ideas

Plants give people good ideas.

Stilt houses copy mangrove trees.
People build their houses on wooden piles
or stilts to keep the houses above water.
A mangrove tree is supported by its
tall roots in just the same way.

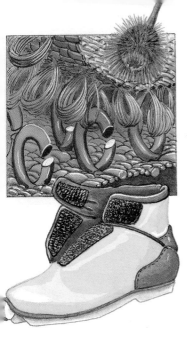

Burdock was the model for Velcro fastenings: its burrs have tiny spines that hook onto other things.

A helicopter flies with its blades spinning – like the winged fruits of a maple tree.

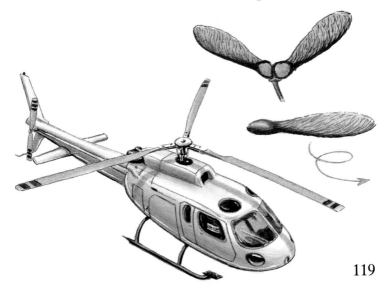

Amazing facts

Some modern medicines are made with synthetic, or man-made, chemicals. But before these were invented, people always used plants.

Many of the medicines used to treat coughs and colds contain oil from the eucalyptus tree.

Rubber used to be made from the latex of the rubber tree, which grows in tropical countries. Latex is a milky white juice in the bark. Nowadays, most rubber is made from synthetic chemicals.

Cotton thread comes from the seed coverings of the cotton plant. China grows more cotton than any other country.

The first plant in Space was Arabidopsis, grown on board the Soviet spacecraft Salyut 7 in 1982.

INDEX